# IF YOU MEET A
# VETERAN

# IF YOU MEET A
# VETERAN

## Written and Illustrated
## by Greg Easley

Liberty Hill Press
2301 Lucien Way #415
Maitland, FL 32751
407.339.4217
www.libertyhillpublishing.com

Printed in the United States of America.

ISBN-13: 978-1-6312-9947-6
Hard Cover: 978-1-6312-9948-3
Ebook: 978-1-6312-9949-0

I dedicate this book to all of those who
answered the call.

# Acknowledgment

I would like to thank my beautiful wife, Erin, and my parents, Ron and Katie, for encouraging me to take on this project. I would also like to thank my two lovely daughters, Olivia and Harper, for inspiring me by watching how quickly they could put a smile on the face of any veteran they met. Lastly, I would like to thank all of the veterans I have had the honor of meeting since I was a child. You were giants to me back then, and you remain that way. I would like to offer a special thank you to my friends at Pampa, Texas' VFW Post 1657.

Next time you go out shopping
Or out with your family to eat

Have a look around the store
And walking down the street

You might just see a man or woman
Shopping or out for a stroll

And if they're wearing a veteran's patch
There's something you should know

That person is called a veteran
Which is a wonderful thing to be

For they once served in uniform
To keep us safe and free

And if you meet a veteran
The very best thing to do

Is shake their hand as firm as you can
And give them a simple "thank you!"

When that veteran was younger
They did what few would do

And set aside their normal life
To serve us, brave and true!

They might have served in the Army
As valiant as a knight

Or in the fearsome Marine Corps
Forever "first to fight"

They might have served in our Navy
Across the oceans wide

Or in the mighty Air Force
Our guardians soaring high

They might have served in the Coast Guard
To the rescue, day or night

Whichever branch they call their own
They wear their patch with pride

If you meet a veteran
Always let them know you care

About the things they had to miss
While they were "over there"

They left behind their loved ones
And said "goodbye" to home

They spent long months so far away
And often felt alone

If you meet a veteran
Man or woman, young or old

22

Always let that person know
That they are your hero

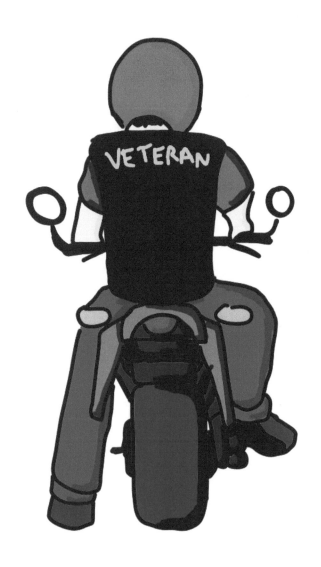

And if you meet a veteran
Don't forget that thanks they're owed

They deserve to feel appreciation
Each time that they are told

Your neighbor, your coach, that man
in the store

Your pilot, or that officer – he served in
the Corps!

Wherever you go you'll see one or two
Just look for those patches and the red,
white, and blue

What an honor to meet a veteran
What a privilege to shake their hand

To let them know their service
Was for a grateful land!

# Questions to Discuss

1.   Who are some of the veterans either in our family or that we know from around town?

2.   What are the five branches of the US Armed Forces?

3.   What are some reasons that you think some men and women decide to serve in our Armed Forces?

4.   Many of our veterans have participated in wars, which must have been a scary experience for them. What do you think helped them find the courage to do their job even when they faced fear?

5.    If you were going to be in our Armed Forces and got to choose, would you rather be in an airplane high above the clouds, on a ship in the ocean, in a submarine deep beneath the waves, or in a tank rolling over hills?

6.    Joining our Armed Forces involves a lot of training and learning. Why do you think our military people need so much practice to do their jobs?

7.    Being in the Armed Forces means learning to follow your leaders' instructions and eventually learning to lead others. Are you a good leader? Do you know any good leaders? What makes someone a good leader?

8.    Being in the Armed Forces isn't only about fighting. Our Armed Forces have

often helped people in our country and in other countries after a natural disaster like a hurricane or a tsunami has caused damage. Why do you think our military is good at helping people in danger?

9.  Several of the illustrations showed members of our Armed Forces carrying different types of weapons. Why do you think it is important for them, or even for those not in the military, to learn how to safely keep, maintain, and handle weapons?

10.  Superheroes from comic books and movies are cool, but veterans are REAL heroes. What about our veterans makes them heroic?

# Take it a Step Further

1.    Get to know those at your local VFW (Veterans of Foreign Wars) Post. Learn what they do, what events they organize, and find out how you can volunteer to help.

2.    Visit any nearby military history museums. Find out all you can and ask questions about volunteering to help the museum.

3.    Many of our older veterans live in retirement or assisted living homes. Get into touch with their office and ask about veterans residing there and plan an event to bring them some cheer. Consider making

Christmas cards for them or performing a song or play for them.

4. Many veterans are buried in cemeteries around the country. Find out about opportunities to volunteer to place flags on important holidays or clean and maintain their grave markers.

5. Ask a veteran if they would be comfortable talking about their experiences or if you could conduct an interview. Some of them prefer to keep their experiences private, and that is fine, but many of them would love that someone is interested in their life story. By interviewing a local veteran you are actively preserving history!

6. There are many charities around the country which help take care of our

veterans, but they rely upon donations to do their work. Get into touch with a charity and find out if you can help them fundraise to make a donation so that they can help even more veterans.

7.   Hospitals, especially VA hospitals, often take care of veterans who are sick. Get into touch with hospital administration and ask about any veterans in their care. Think of some ways you could put a smile on their face. Consider writing them get well soon cards or drawing them encouraging pictures.

8.   Ask your teacher if there would be a good time for you to share with your classmates what you have learned about veterans. Some of your classmates might not know about what a veteran is or why they are so important, and it could give

you a chance to let them know they have real-life heroes in your own neighborhood.

9.   If you see a veteran eating alone at a restaurant, ask them if they'd like to join your family or consider telling your server you'd like to pay for their meal.

10.   Cherish this country and what it stands for. Learn about the principles our country was founded upon that make it special. As you grow up, consider actively participating through voting and helping in your community. Be the kind of citizen that our veterans have always been proud to defend.

11.   If you think you might like to join the Armed Forces when you grow up, speak to an adult you trust about it, or speak to a veteran and ask for their advice. If

joining becomes your goal, work toward it by learning as much as you can in all of your classes, eating healthy, and staying active in outdoor activities or sports to be physically healthy.

Photo Challenge! Next time you get to meet a veteran ask an adult to snap a picture and send it to IfYouMeetAVeteran@gmail.com

We would love to feature your photo with a veteran on our social media page!

CPSIA information can be obtained
at www.ICGtesting.com
Printed in the USA
LVHW071147130920
665868LV00012B/1044